THE CHATGPT MILLIONAIRE

MAKING MONEY ONLINE HAS NEVER BEEN
THIS EASY

NEIL DAGGER

CONTENTS

Your FREE Bonus   v

Introduction   vii

1. That's great and all - but what can I use ChatGPT   1
   for?

2. Getting Started with ChatGPT   5

3. Here are a few tips for using ChatGPT effectively: 10

4. Experience Skyrocketing Productivity Growth   16
   with ChatGPT

5. Use ChatGPT to Create Passive Income Streams   46
   that Keep on Giving

6. Become a superhuman freelancer with ChatGPT   78

7. "Act as" prompts - My favourites   87

8. Limitations   100

9. Conclusions   102

Thank You!   105

YOUR FREE BONUS

As an additional BONUS you for your purchase, I'd like to give you two gifts:

BONUS 1: 150+ Powerful prompts

These are "copy and paste" prompts that you can start using immediately to get amazing results from ChatGPT. This is in addition to the prompts shown in this book.

BONUS 2: "The simple guide to wealth"

You may know that 70% of lottery winners go broke within 6 years. It's because they don't understand the secrets of how to maintain and grow money into generational wealth.

This guide will teach you these secrets, along with how to apply them to your new found ChatGPT income.

Get both free gifts now, here:

https://retiredecadesearly.com/bonus

Alternatively, scan the QR code below:

If you have any issues, disable your browser's adblocker for this page. If that doesn't work, you can email me at Neil@retiredecadesearly.com

Tools I used to write this book (aside from ChatGPT)

JasperAI: JasperGPT.com

INTRODUCTION

As I write this, ChatGPT is already the fastest-growing tech platform ever - **hitting a million users in just 5 days**. For comparison, this took Netflix 3 years, Twitter 2 years, Facebook 10 months and Instagram 2.5 months.

Update in March 2023, it's now the fastest platform to hit 100 million users!

I think that ChatGPT is going to be revolutionary, and I wanted this introduction to make you, the reader, feel as excited as I am about this, so I decided to use ChatGPT to help; I asked it to create an introduction for this book in the style of **Steve Jobs** and here's what it came up with (after a little editing).

"Welcome to the revolutionary world of **ChatGPT - a powerful language model that has the potential to transform the way you make money.**

This book is a guide to unlocking the true potential of Chat-

GPT, showing you how to harness its advanced capabilities to generate income and grow your business.

With ChatGPT, you can automate tedious tasks, streamline workflows, and create new revenue streams. **It's not just a tool, it's a companion that can help you achieve financial success."**

From creating engaging content and generating complex code to customer service and performing research, the possibilities are endless. **This book will teach you how to use ChatGPT to create new opportunities, save time, and improve your bottom line.**

This book is not just for entrepreneurs and business owners but also for anyone looking to monetise their skills and talents using ChatGPT.

As a freelancer, a digital marketer or a content creator, you will learn how to use ChatGPT to improve your productivity and income.

So, whether you're looking to start a business, grow an existing one, or simply increase your income, this book is for you.

Let ChatGPT be your guide to financial success, and let's start the journey to becoming a ChatGPT millionaire.

THAT'S GREAT AND ALL - BUT WHAT CAN I USE CHATGPT FOR?

YES, well, to get to the crux of the matter, you can

Generate leads and write cold outreach emails

How many times have you started at a blank e-mail or direct message, wondering how exactly to reach out to a potential client completely cold?

ChatGPT can instantly generate e-mails or messages for any given situation and allow you to reach more potential customers faster.

Boost your online visibility

Everyone needs to have an online presence these days, But this is a time-consuming task, social media platforms have different types of content you need to put on them, and you can't just copy and paste your LinkedIn post on Twitter.

Some companies pay thousands of dollars a month, paying dedicated social media managers. ChatGPT can instantly create your social media content so you can reach more potential customers while saving money and time.

It is especially powerful when you want to get your content out to multiple platforms on social media, as it allows you to repurpose content instantly from one platform to another. We'll go over this in depth in **Chapter 4.**

Create lasting ties with your clients

Have you ever hired a freelancer that took forever to finish your job, asked for multiple clarifications and took ages to reply? Even if the quality were great, you'd never use them again if you had an urgent task.

Now imagine that using ChatGPT, you were able to generate the same quality work at 10x the speed of your competitors - they'll come back to you over and over again!

Create new revenue streams

As a business owner or entrepreneur, you always have a lot of things on your to-do list. You may want to start a blog, create a new product or just build /update your website, but these things take time and money, too if you can't do them yourself.

ChatGPT can help you create new products or features that you may have thought weren't possible for you because of the amount of time or the type of skill set required, but now you can do these things yourself and at a much faster pace.

If you're looking to create passive income

streams, there's a full chapter dedicated to that (Chapter 5)

Determine the best pricing structure

Once you've created a product, you want to obviously make sure you're getting the maximum profit possible, but you also don't want to alienate potential customers.

People spend a lot of time trying to get the balance right, but finding the exact data can be tricky; there are many things to consider, from the type of product, demographics, and channels to your competitors and your budget.

ChatGPT can provide insights on pricing strategies, consumer buying habits, and guidance on adjusting pricing for optimal results - since it's trained on information that includes thousands of studies, books, and business articles, it's like getting tailored expert advice.

Utilise new tools and technologies

New tools and technologies are popping up every day, and no matter what kind of work you do, there will be lots of them you'll be unaware of that can save you a lot of time, but researching them is tricky; everyone wants to sell you their product and searching online it's almost impossible to get a result that's just right for you.

ChatGPT can suggest and help you implement new tools and workflows that automate various menial tasks so you can have more time to focus on what really matters to you.

Anything else you've always wanted to do but thought it would take too long

- Want to start a blog but don't have the patience to write multiple blog posts every week?
- Want to create a YouTube channel but don't have the time to plan your scripts?
- Want to start learning to code, finally?
- Want to learn a new language?
- Want to help your kid study?

All of these things became much easier and faster to do with ChatGPT.

So get started now.

GETTING STARTED WITH CHATGPT

Step 1: Sign up for an OpenAI account

GO to chat.openai.com and sign up for an OpenAI account. This will allow you to access ChatGPT.

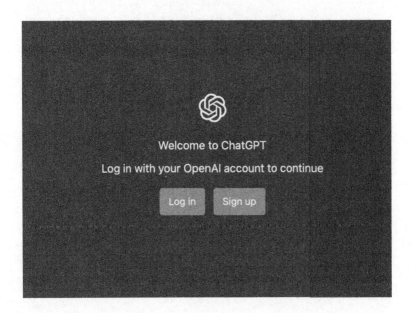

To sign up for an account, simply visit the OpenAI website and click the "Sign Up" button on the page and then create an account. You will need to provide some basic information, such as your name and email address, and agree to the terms of service. Once you have completed the sign-up process, you will be able to log in with your new account.

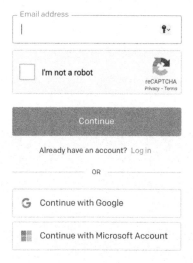

Step 2: Explore the ChatGPT model

Once you have logged in to chat.openai.com, you will be able to explore the ChatGPT model by typing a prompt into the input field and clicking the "Send" button. ChatGPT will then generate a response based on your prompt.

You can experiment with different prompts and settings to see how ChatGPT responds. For example, you can try to specify different lengths and tones to see how it affects the randomness and creativity of the generated text.

Step 3: (Optional) Choosing your GPT Model (Paid accounts only)

When you sign up for ChatGPT, you have the option to upgrade to "ChatGPT Plus" - it costs 20 USD per month, and one of the main benefits is that you can use ChatGPT even if the free version of ChatGPT is at capacity.

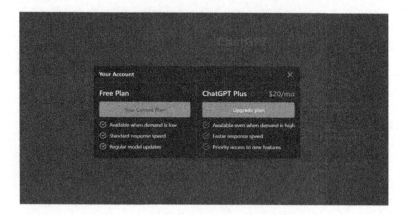

If you're paying for ChatGPT Plus, you'll notice something new with the release of **GPT-4**; at the top of the page, you'll see a drop-down box where you'll be able to choose from different models. For the **best results,** you should choose **GPT-4,** bearing in mind that it'll be a bit slower and it has a messaging limit (25 messages per 3 hours)

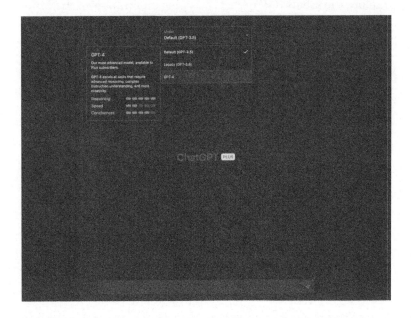

Step 4: ChatGPT in Action

The image below shows me asking the prompt: "Tell me 7 interesting facts about you."

This is the chatGPT screen; if you haven't already, go to chat.openai.com and play around with it.

Start with a simple "Hi," ask it questions, ask it to code stuff or ask it to translate or analyse stuff, generate book summaries and book recommendations, and ask it what to ask ChatGPT itself.

3

HERE ARE A FEW TIPS FOR USING CHATGPT EFFECTIVELY:

Set a clear goal and be precise in what you ask

THIS IS PROBABLY the most important part you need to learn to ensure that the responses you get from ChatGPT are exactly what you need, and it'll take some practice. When you ask ChatGPT something, it's called a "Prompt".

For example, let's say you're planning a day trip to London, and you want to sight-see; you'd use:

Prompt: *I'm going on a day trip to London, give me some places to visit for sightseeing*

ChatGPT Response:

Absolutely! London is a beautiful city with many amazing places to see. Here are some suggestions for your day trip:

1. The British Museum
2. The Tower of London

3. The Houses of Parliament and Big Ben
4. Buckingham Palace
5. The London Eye
6. Trafalgar Square
7. St. Paul's Cathedral

Note: ChatGPT also gave two lines of description for each of these attractions, but I've removed them to keep it short.

As you can see, it gave me a very standard, touristy response, but if you've been to London before or you don't want to go to crowded, well-known places, you can ask:

Prompt: Tell me some lesser-known but still interesting places instead.

ChatGPT Response:

Sure, here are some lesser-known but still interesting places to check out during your day trip to London:

1. Leadenhall Market
2. Sir John Soane's Museum
3. The Old Operating Theatre Museum
4. Highgate Cemetery
5. The Hunterian Museum
6. Dennis Severs' House
7. The Grant Museum of Zoology

I hope these suggestions help you discover some hidden gems in London!

Now, the list is entirely different, but there are three museums on the list, and I'm not a big fan, so I typed:

Prompt: I'm not a big fan of museums

ChatGPT response:

No problem, there are still many interesting places to visit in London that don't involve museums! Here are some ideas:

1. Camden Market
2. Brick Lane
3. Greenwich
4. Notting Hill
5. The South Bank
6. The Sky Garden
7. Little Venice

Two things to note here.

Firstly, the results have changed completely based on how the question was asked, and it learnt more about what I wanted with each new prompt - telling it I didn't like museums changed the whole list - rather than just replacing the museums.

The results would have been different if I said, "I like plays" or "I like shopping", in addition to the original prompt.

Second, we didn't have to re-phrase the whole question each time; it just understood that we were still talking about sightseeing in London. This is what makes ChatGPT so powerful.

Experiment

Don't be afraid to test different prompts and settings. You never know; you might find a new way to generate the content you never thought of before. When creating content, you can ask, **"Write this in a witty, funny, engaging tone"**, or you can even ask it to write something **a specific person would** like **", Write this podcast introduction in the style of Joe Rogan."**

The "Act as" hack

This is the ultimate technique to get unique, personalised and valuable content from chatGPT for particular situations by copying and pasting the text in italics; <u>you can try out this example below:</u>

Prompt: *"I want you to act as a novelist. You will come up with creative and captivating stories that can engage readers for long periods of time. You may choose any genre such as fantasy, romance, or historical fiction, but the aim is to write something with an outstanding plot line, engaging characters and unexpected climaxes. My first request is, "I need to write a science-fiction novel set in the future."*

Chapter 7 has a list of my favourite "Act As" Prompts.

Regenerate response

When you get a response from ChatGPT but aren't entirely happy with it - you can click on the "Regenerate response" box - it'll remove the current output and create a whole new one. Sometimes it may give you an error because it's overloaded - you can use the "Regenerate response" option for this situation again.

Get multiple responses for the same query

This is especially useful if you want to pick stuff like email subjects or video/blog titles; you're unlikely to get one you LOVE on the first try, so you can ask chatGPT to generate 5,10 or even 20 responses in one go.

Example: Please generate ten engaging blog post titles for an article about the new features of the latest iPhone.

Refine and edit

While ChatGPT is an excellent tool for generating high-quality content, it's not a substitute for human editing. Take the time to review and refine the generated text to ensure it's error-free and meets the needs of your business. You can even input existing text - anything from emails and blog posts to a book chapter to ChatGPT and ask it to "Give me Suggestions to improve this", and it'll do it - you can focus on things like clarity, readability, and tone too.

e.g. Please provide suggestions to improve the readability and make this email more professional.

. . .

With these tips in mind and by experimenting, you can harness the full potential of ChatGPT to create content that truly resonates with your audience and drives success for you.

Don't forget: Your FREE bonus allows you to access a list of over 150 "Act as" prompts for various scenarios, so grab it.

https://retiredecadesearly.com/bonus

4

EXPERIENCE SKYROCKETING PRODUCTIVITY GROWTH WITH CHATGPT

IF YOU'RE AN ENTREPRENEUR, a freelancer, a start-up or even a small company, you're often a one-man band who has to either learn how to do a lot of different things, which takes forever or outsource the work as it comes - which works but is expensive and there's a lack of continuity should the same type of work come around again and the freelancer you used last time is not available.

With ChatGPT, these problems are (mostly) a thing of the past, whatever skillset you may want to employ, copywriting, coding, creating art, creating ads, creating blog content, writing books, SEO? All of this and more can be done by ChatGPT; you just have to use the right prompt.

This will massively cut down on your time spent worrying about the mundane aspects of the business and allow you to just get on with the important things you need to focus on.

For certain examples, I'll be showing full responses from ChatGPT just to show how much the output can change depending on your prompt.

Cold outreach emails

How long does it take you to write the perfect cold outreach email? Have you ever spent hours searching for a perfect email template that applies to your situation and industry but couldn't?

You need to now, write it yourself, and you have to:

- Be clear and concise: Get to the point quickly, and explain the value of what you offer and why it would benefit them.
- Make it scannable: Use headings, bullet points, and short paragraphs to make the email easy to read.
- Add Credibility: Provide any necessary credentials or references and statistics that can be used to support your offer or idea.
- Show a clear call to action: Be direct and specific in what you would like the recipient to do, whether setting up a call, getting them to visit a website or trying out a product.
- Proofread and Edit: Review your message carefully for grammar, punctuation, and typos.
- Add a clear subject line: Make sure the subject line is attention-grabbing, specific and shows the purpose of the email.

But now, taking ages to painstakingly craft an email is a thing of the past.

Say you're an estate agency, that wants to send an email to a potential client, all you have to do is ask.

Example: Cold outreach emails for your business (e.g. Estate agency)

Prompt: Write a cold outreach email for *my estate agency to a prospective landlord.*

ChatGPT response:

Dear [Prospective Landlord],

I hope this email finds you well. My name is [Your Name] and I'm the owner of [Estate Agency]. I wanted to take a moment to introduce myself and our agency to you.

At [Estate Agency], we pride ourselves on being a modern and forward-thinking agency that puts our clients' needs first. Our team is dedicated to helping landlords like you find the perfect tenants for your properties and providing top-notch service throughout the process.

We have a wealth of experience in the industry and a track record of successful rentals. We believe that clear communication and attention to detail are key to building strong landlord-tenant relationships and ensuring a smooth rental process.

If you're interested in learning more about how we can work together, we'd love to schedule a call to discuss your specific needs and answer any questions you may have.

Thank you for considering [Estate Agency] for your rental needs. I look forward to potentially working with you.

Best regards,

[Your Name]

This is pretty usable, you can make some tweaks but if you're someone who struggles with what exactly to write - it's a great starting point.

Now, I'll give you another example of a cold outreach email to show just how easy it is to change the prompt slightly and make it relevant to a different business type.

Example: Cold outreach emails for your business (e.g. Foreign exchange advisory firm)

A friend of mine owns an FX advisory firm, and he was struggling to find suitable email templates for cold outreach, he spent ages trying to find one but couldn't find one that was both customisable and appropriate - when we spoke about it, I'd just found ChatGPT and with it, I was able to help him create one in less than a minute and he was so happy with it I decided to write a book on how useful ChatGPT can be.

Prompt: Write a **professional** cold outreach email for a Foreign exchange advisory firm to a prospective client.

ChatGPT response:

Subject: Secure your Business's Financial Success with [Company Name]'s Foreign Exchange Expertise

Dear [Client],

My name is [Your Name] and I am the founder of [Your Company, a foreign exchange advisory firm.

I wanted to reach out to you because I believe that we may be able to help your business navigate the often volatile and complex world of foreign exchange. As you may know, small fluctuations in currency exchange rates can have a big impact on the bottom line of any business, particularly those that operate internationally.

At [Your Company, we offer a range of services designed to help our clients manage their foreign exchange risk and take advantage of opportunities as they arise. These services include market analysis, currency hedging, and trade execution, among others.

I would love the opportunity to discuss how we may be able to assist your business in more detail. Could we schedule a call at a convenient time for you to discuss this further?

Thank you for considering our services. I look forward to speaking with you soon.

Best regards,

[Your name]

This is decent, especially if you're struggling, but we can improve it.

Example: Make it more engaging and personal

Prompt: Make the e-mail more engaging and personal

ChatGPT Response:

Subject: Discover the Foreign Exchange Edge Your Business Needs with [Company Name]

Dear [Recipient's name],

I hope this email finds you well and that your business is thriving. My name is [Your Name], and as the founder of [Company

Name], a leading foreign exchange advisory firm, I know all too well how the global currency market can make or break a business.

That's why I want to personally reach out to you today and offer my team's expertise to help you navigate the ever-changing world of foreign exchange and position your business for success.

At [Company Name], we specialize in helping businesses like yours identify opportunities and manage currency risk. Our team of experts is dedicated to providing our clients with in-depth market analysis, customized risk management strategies, and real-time trading insights to ensure you're always ahead of the curve.

I'd love the opportunity to have a more in-depth conversation with you about your specific foreign exchange needs and how we can help you achieve your financial goals. Let's schedule a quick call next week and discuss this further.

Thank you for your time, and I hope to hear from you soon.

Best regards,

[Your Name]

PS: I also would love to share some of our recent client testimonials if you're interested.

This version of the email has a more personal and engaging tone. There's a genuine interest in the recipient's business and well-being, and chatGPT uses personal pronouns to address them directly. The email also ended with a friendly PS, this way the writer is being less formal and shows a more friendly side of the company.

As you can imagine, this works with any type of business, you can modify the prompt to get a different answer, and you can modify the parameters to make it funnier or more engaging, give it a personality trait that you think would be more likely to get a response - you can even use different **author styles**.

Example: Write a cold approach email In the style of Elon Musk

Prompt: Rewrite that cold approach email in the style of Elon musk

ChatGPT Response:

It's important to note that the way Elon Musk communicates, especially in cold approach emails, may not align with a professional or formal tone, and in some cases, may not be the most appropriate approach. Also, the content, style, and tone of the email will depend on the audience that the email is intended for. With that in mind here is a possible version:

Subject: Revolutionising the Foreign Exchange Market with [Company Name]

Yo [Recipient's name],

It's [Your Name], the founder of [Company Name], the future of foreign exchange advisory.

I bet you're tired of traditional firms that are not equipped to handle the rapidly changing market. Let me tell you, we're different. We're not just in the business of managing currency risk, we're in the business of creating opportunities, and we're damn good at it.

Our team of experts is dedicated to providing our clients with in-depth market analysis, customised risk management strategies, and real-time trading insights that will put you light-years ahead of the competition.

We're the kind of firm that's not afraid to think differently and go against the status quo.

We're inviting you to experience a free consultation with one of our advisors, and I guarantee you'll see the difference. Let's schedule a call, and let's change the game.

Regards,

[Your Name]

Example: Customer service emails and template creation

You can use this as a live tool to answer emails as well as create templates that your customer service can use for a specific query type. I'll give below the example of a user asking for a refund but that is against your store policy.

Prompt: Write a polite but firm email to a customer that is asking for a refund, but company policy is no refunds.

ChatGPT response:

Dear [Customer],

Thank you for your email regarding your recent purchase with our company. We apologize for any dissatisfaction you may have experienced with your purchase.

After reviewing our company policy, I regret to inform you that we are unable to process a refund for your purchase.

Our policy states that we do not offer refunds for any reason.

We understand that this may not be the outcome you were hoping for, and we apologize for any inconvenience this may cause.

If you have any further concerns or questions, please do not hesitate to contact us.

Thank you for your understanding.

Sincerely,

[Your Name]

Blog posts

Let's say you want to write an engaging blog post for your audience, but creating a high-quality blog post is hard work that takes quite a long time, you have to:

- Choose a topic that is both interesting and relevant to your target audience
- Conduct thorough research on your chosen topic using reputable sources
- Organise the information you've gathered into a logical structure using headings, subheadings, bullet points, and numbered lists
- Write a clear and compelling introduction using an engaging and conversational tone

- Edit and proofread for grammar, spelling, and clarity, and make sure to properly cite sources
- Optimise posts for search engines using keywords and meta descriptions
- Publish the post, share it on social media and other platforms, and encourage comments and feedback to create engagement with the audience.

But a lot of that work can now be done for you, at the click of a button.

Example: Ideas for a Blog post in your niche using keywords that have high search volume but low competition

Prompt: Give me 5 blog post ideas for high search volume and low competition keywords for drones.

ChatGPT response:

Here are five potential blog post ideas for high search volume and low competition keywords related to drones:

- "The Beginner's Guide to Flying Drones: Tips and Tricks for First-Time Pilots"
- "Top 10 Affordable Drones for Capturing Stunning Aerial Photos and Videos"
- "How to Choose the Best Drone for Your Needs: A Comprehensive Buying Guide"
- "The Legalities of Drone Flying: Understanding FAA Regulations and Best Practices"
- "From Racing to Mapping: The Surprising Ways Drones Are Being Used in Industries Today"

Example: Writing a blog post outline

So, say that you liked number 4 and wanted to write a post. Here's what to do, you can ask it to create an outline (which you can later use to generate the whole blog - I'll show this in the next example)

Prompt: Write a 7-paragraph outline for a blog post with the title "The Legalities of Drone Flying: Understanding FAA Regulations and Best Practices"

ChatGPT response:

I. Introduction

- Definition of drones and their increasing popularity
- Importance of understanding and following FAA regulations for drone flying

II. Overview of FAA regulations for drones

- Small UAS Rule (Part 107)
- Registration requirements
- Safety guidelines

III. Operating a drone for hobby or recreation

- Guidelines for flying drones for hobby or recreation
- Responsibility of hobbyist drone pilots

IV. Operating a drone for commercial purposes

- Requirements for obtaining a Remote Pilot Certificate
- Operating rules for commercial drone pilots

V. Privacy considerations for drone flying

- FAA guidelines on privacy
- State and local laws on drone privacy

VI. Flying drones near airports and aircraft

- FAA guidelines on flying drones near airports and aircraft
- Potential consequences for violating these guidelines

VII. Insurance considerations for drone pilots

- Types of insurance available for drone operators
- Importance of carrying insurance for liability purposes

Example: Writing a blog post

Now using the blog outline above, we can ask it to generate a full blog post. It's important to structure it like this rather than asking it to create it in one go since you can then easily restructure the blog as you see fit and allow the AI to form a more coherent structure.

Prompt: Use the above outline to create an in-depth detailed blog post with SEO already applied.

ChatGPT response:

The Legalities of Drone Flying: Understanding FAA Regulations and Best Practices

Drones have become increasingly popular in recent years for a variety of purposes, from capturing aerial footage for film-making to performing inspections for construction companies.

But with the rise of drone usage comes the need for regulations to ensure safety and compliance.

In this blog post, we'll delve into the legalities of drone flying, with a specific focus on the regulations set forth by the Federal Aviation Administration (FAA) and best practices for flying drones safely and legally.

Understanding FAA Regulations for Drones

The FAA is responsible for regulating the airspace in the United States and therefore has specific regulations in place for drones. These regulations include rules for registration, flight restrictions, and operation guidelines.

(*N.B. I haven't included the whole blog output here as it would take up too much space*)

This is factually correct but a bit dry, so I decided to give it another prompt once it finished:

Prompt: Please make it funnier and make the tone informal

ChatGPT Response:

"Ready to soar like a bird and snap some seriously cool aerial footage? Or maybe you're thinking of starting your own drone-based business delivering pizzas or inspecting wind turbines.

Whatever your drone-flying dreams may be, there's one thing you absolutely have to do before you take to the skies: Learn the legalities. Because, let's face it, getting into hot water with the Feds isn't exactly the most exhilarating way to fly.

First things first, the Federal Aviation Administration (FAA) is the big kahuna when it comes to regulating drones in the US. They have a bunch of rules and regulations you need to know before you start buzzing around like a fly on steroids. These include registration requirements, flight restrictions, and operating guidelines. It's important to get familiar with these regulations, otherwise, you might end up with a hefty fine, or worse, in prison.

I cut off the rest of the blog - but you can see how this is a lot more readable, you may see that it's lost the SEO formatting but it's simple enough to give another prompt to say "Please add the headings and SEO formatting to this" and it'll do it.

(You can see the basic idea, you can change the prompt and use it to create a blog for any topic! If you need more detail or if the script generated isn't long enough, you can just type "please rewrite it to be longer with more detail on [topic]")

Youtube/Podcast script

If you've ever created a youtube video or a podcast, you know the amount of work that goes into it before you even start recording, you have to:

- Write a compelling introduction to hook the viewer
- Organize the script into a logical structure with headings and subheadings
- Use simple and easy-to-understand language
- Create a call-to-action at the end of the video to subscribe to your channel
- Rehearse, edit and optimize the script for SEO

- Keep it consistent with the tone, language, and message of your channel
- Make sure to have a clear message that resonates with your target audience

Example: Creating a Script for a Youtube video or your podcast

Now let's say you're trying to build your social media presence and you want to use the blog article you created and generate a video/podcast out of it.

You can use the already existing content you generated for a blog outline and turn it into a script that you can then read out!

Prompt: Using the blog outline above for The Legalities of Drone Flying: Understanding FAA Regulations and Best Practices", please create a step-by-step, detailed and engaging youtube video script.

ChatGPT Response:

"Hi and welcome to our channel! If you're interested in operating a drone, it's important to understand the legalities and best practices for doing so. That's what we'll be discussing in today's video.

First, let's start with the basics of FAA regulation. In the United States, the Federal Aviation Administration is responsible for regulating drones. If your drone weighs more than 0.55 pounds, or 250 grams, it must be registered with the FAA. This includes the weight of the drone itself, as well as any additional payloads or equipment.

(*N.B. I haven't put the whole script here, you can change the prompt and use it to create a video script for any topic! If you need more detail or if the script generated isn't long enough, you can just type "please rewrite it to be longer with more detail on [topic]"*)

Social media marketing

In this day and age, social media marketing is a must for any entrepreneur or business owner.

Whether you manage your social media marketing or work at an agency, it's very competitive.

These are just some of the challenges you face :

- Keeping up with all the algorithm changes on social media platforms can be a real headache. You never know what's gonna work and what's not, so you gotta be quick on your feet and adapt your strategies.
- Staying on top of the latest trends and innovations in social media marketing is a must. The field is always changing and you don't wanna fall behind.
- Coming up with engaging content that resonates with your target audience is a toughie. You gotta make sure it's shareable, on-brand and hits the mark.
- Measuring the ROI of social media campaigns can be a real challenge. It's hard to put a number on the impact of social media efforts on a business's bottom line.
- Managing client expectations can be tricky. They may have unrealistic expectations or may not fully understand the ins and outs of social media marketing.

- Managing a team can be a real challenge as your agency grows. Social media professionals can be a handful.
- Balancing creativity and strategy is key. You gotta come up with creative and engaging content that also supports a client's business goals.
- Staying within budget while delivering results for clients can be a real challenge.
- Dealing with negative comments and criticism is just a part of the job, but it can be tough to handle.

For example, let's say you run a digital marketing agency and you're always on the lookout for fresh content to share with your clients.

By leveraging ChatGPT to produce professional-grade content, you can increase conversions and drive sales for your clients and ultimately your business.

We'll look at a way here to quickly create content for multiple social media channels.

Example: Creating a complete marketing campaign

You want to pitch an advertising campaign to a client on the spot - they want to launch a new energy drink and want a breakdown of what the campaign would look like and approximate costs.

So let's create a marketing campaign using the "Act as" prompt.

Prompt: I want you to act as an advertising agency. You will create a full and detailed marketing campaign to promote a product or service of your choice. You will choose a target audience, develop key messages and slogans, select the media channels for promotion, and decide on any additional activities needed to reach your goals. Give examples of the cost of advertising in each social media channel, as well as the best estimate of CPM and CPC charges. My first request is "I need help creating an advertising campaign for a new type of energy drink targeting young adults aged 18-30."

ChatGPT Response:

Advertising Campaign for New Energy Drink

Target audience: Young adults aged 18-30

Key messages:

- A new type of energy drink that delivers a unique combination of caffeine, vitamins, and natural ingredients
- Designed to give you the energy boost you need without the crash
- Perfect for young adults who lead an active lifestyle
- Slogan: "Fuel your energy, fuel your life"
- Media channels:
- Social media (Instagram, Facebook, and TikTok)
- Online streaming platforms (YouTube, Twitch)
- Outdoor advertising (billboards, posters)

Cost estimates:

Social media advertising:

- Instagram: $0.50-$2.00 per click, $5-$15 CPM
- Facebook: $0.50-$2.00 per click, $5-$15 CPM
- TikTok: $0.50-$2.00 per click, $5-$15 CPM

Online streaming platforms:

- YouTube: $0.10-$0.30 per view, $5-$15 CPM
- Twitch: $0.10-$0.30 per view, $5-$15 CPM

Outdoor advertising:

- Billboards: $2,000-$20,000 per month
- Posters: $500-$5,000 per month

Activities:

- Influencer marketing partnerships with popular fitness and lifestyle influencers
- Product samplings at fitness events and college campuses
- Interactive social media contests and giveaways
- In-store displays and promotions
- Sponsorship of local sports teams or events."

This is a pretty decent starting point, it gives you a slog, the key messages as well as an overview of the platforms and channels to use, approximate costs and activities as well as costs - pretty useful. You can amend the prompt to ask for timelines as well as give costs for other channels or even ask it to allocate a budget based on the best Return on investment.

Example: Social media post - Instagram

Let's imagine your client is launching a subscription box service that delivers curated eco-friendly and sustainable products every month. Products that are included in the box include reusable straws, beeswax wraps, and zero-waste cleaning products.

So to create an Instagram post for this service:

Prompt: As a marketing agency Create an engaging Instagram post for the subscription box service

ChatGPT Response:

"Switching to a sustainable lifestyle just got a whole lot easier! Introducing our eco-friendly subscription box service - delivering curated, earth-friendly products straight to your doorstep every month. From reusable straws and beeswax wraps, to zero-waste cleaning products, our box is the perfect way to discover new sustainable products and make a positive impact on the planet.

Our box is not just about the products, it is about the experience of living more sustainably, every day and we make it easy for you to transition. Whether you're a seasoned eco-warrior or just starting your sustainability journey, our subscription box is perfect for anyone looking to make a change.

You don't have to worry about traveling to different shops or searching the internet to find sustainable products anymore. Just subscribe, sit back, and let us handle the rest.

Want to join the eco-friendly revolution? Sign up now and get 25% off your first box with the code 'GO GREEN'! #sustainability #ecofriendly #subscriptionbox"

The post can feature a clean and attractive set of product images or video to showcase the eco-friendly products. It provides a clear Call-to-action and a sense of urgency with a limited time offer. The post's hashtags will also help to increase visibility to audiences interested in eco-friendly and sustainability.

Now normally a company like this would want to have a presence on all social media platforms, and normally to create a post on something like Twitter you'd have to start from scratch because the medium is so different and the character limit is a challenge too.

But now you can just ask ChatGPT to do it for you. Example below:

Example: Re-purposed Social media post - Twitter

Prompt: Now, As a marketing agency, re-purpose this into an engaging tweet

ChatGPT Response:

"Want to make an impact for the planet? Subscribe to our eco-friendly subscription box and discover sustainable products every month! #sustainability #ecofriendly #subscriptionbox. Use code 'GO GREEN' for 25% off your first box! 🌐🌿📦 #gogreen"

Twitter's post is shorter than Instagram's post so the message has to be concise and engaging. I tried to keep the essence of the message, highlighting the main benefit of the subscription box and its eco-friendly feature. I also included a call-to-action to subscribe, a promotion and the relevant hashtags to increase visibility. The added emojis are engaging and create a sense of connection with the audience who are interested in green living.

You can carry on doing this, re-purposing the initial post to a Facebook and LinkedIn post or something different like Pinterest or a TikTok video script. This can save a lot of time and also ensure that a consistent tone and branding are used across all platforms with minimal effort.

Let's say you have an e-commerce store selling handmade crafts.

By using ChatGPT to generate product descriptions for Etsy or your store you can increase interest and drive more sales.

You could also use ChatGPT to generate email marketing campaigns that promote your products and offer special discounts or promotions to your subscribers.

It's also a lot easier to create engaging and shareable content for platforms like Pinterest, Twitter, and Instagram, you can reach a wider audience and build a loyal following.

This can be really effective if you're able to tap into trending topics and hashtags, as this can help your content go viral and bring in tons of new traffic and exposure.

Example: Etsy Product description

Prompt: Create an Etsy product listing for a handmade oak chair

ChatGPT Response:

"Handcrafted Oak Chair: A Timeless Design for Your Home

Looking for a chair that's both stylish and durable? Look no further than our handcrafted oak chair! Made from solid oak wood, this chair is built to last and is sure to become a cherished piece in your home.

This chair is handcrafted by skilled artisans who pay attention to every detail.

(N.B. I cut off around 3 paragraphs here - It created a whole page of description despite having very little information to start with)

Example: Linkedin posts

If you have a personal brand focused on health and wellness, let's say you want to increase your LinkedIn following by posting useful information there.

Prompt: In an engaging tone please write a LinkedIn post on the importance of vitamin D

ChatGPT response:

"More Than Just Good for Your Bones: The Surprising Health Benefits of Vitamin D"

Vitamin D, also known as the "sunshine vitamin," is essential for maintaining strong bones and a healthy immune system.

But did you know that it also plays a crucial role in preventing chronic diseases such as cancer, heart disease, and diabetes? Studies have shown that people with low levels of Vitamin D are more likely to develop these conditions.

Stay healthy and sunny! #vitamind #healthylifestyle #nutrition

As you can see it tried to draw the reader in with the "Did you know" - I've cut off part of the output - there were 3 additional paragraphs before the end - but I wanted to show how it ended with hashtags appropriate for LinkedIn.

Diet/Nutrition/Personal Training

If you need a diet plan but don't have the time to do the research and don't want to pay a dietician, you can just ask. You won't need to read up on Carbs, keto, macros, caloric deficit, or any of those things that can take a long time to understand and even longer to create a proper plan tailored to you!

The same goes for exercising, you have to either get a personal trainer or spend hours trying to understand muscle groups and exercise names - it's so tedious, especially when you just want to get on with it!

Here we're going to create a diet plan for an individual and then show why chatGPT is so much more useful than if you'd just googled a diet plan because now, taking into account everything you entered here, including the diet plan, you can ask it to generate a tailored workout regime that takes it all into account!

Example: Tailored diet plan(s)

But with ChatGPT, You can also use this to create custom diet plans for you and if you happen to be a personal trainer, nutritionist or dietician, this will save you hours of research.

Prompt: As a dietician, give me a 2-week diet plan with caloric breakdown for a vegetarian male aged 35 weighing 220 pounds and 6 feet tall. I want to lose 2 pounds a week. Keep the macros at 50% carbs, 15% fats and 35% protein.

ChatGPT response:

Week 1:

Day 1:

- Breakfast: 1 cup oatmeal with 1/2 cup mixed berries and 1 tablespoon of chopped almonds (307 calories)
- Lunch: Grilled vegetable and hummus wrap with lettuce and tomato in a whole grain tortilla (285 calories)
- Dinner: Baked tofu with 1 cup roasted vegetables and 1 cup quinoa (514 calories)
- Snacks: 1 small handful of baby carrots (35 calories), 2 small pieces of dark chocolate (140 calories)
- **Total**: 1271 calories

(*N.B. I haven't put the whole plan here but you can change the prompt and use it to yours/your client's characteristics and their weight loss goals! If it stops after generating part of your diet plan depending on how long you asked for, you can just type "keep going" and it will carry on creating the plan*)

Example: Using context to create Tailored workout plan(s)

Now, all you have to do is allow chatGPT to use the above context and generate not only something tailored to your physique and plans but something that takes into account your diet too.

Prompt: Now, keeping the diet in mind, generate a workout plan for the same individual

ChatGPT Response:

Sure, here is a sample 2-week workout plan for a vegetarian male aged 35 weighing 220 pounds and 6 feet tall, designed to complement the diet plan and help reach the goal of losing 2 pounds per week:

Week 1:

- Monday: Cardio - 30 minutes of steady-state cardio (jogging, cycling, or swimming)
- Tuesday: Strength training - full-body workout (squats, deadlifts, bench press, rows) with 3 sets of 8-12 reps
- Wednesday: Rest
- Thursday: Cardio - 30 minutes of steady-state cardio
- Friday: Strength training - upper body workout (dumbbell press, rows, pull-ups) with 3 sets of 8-12 reps
- Saturday: Cardio - 30 minutes of steady-state cardio
- Sunday: Rest

Week 2:

- Monday: Cardio - 30 minutes of steady-state cardio
- Tuesday: Strength training - full-body workout with 3 sets of 8-12 reps
- Wednesday: Rest
- Thursday: Cardio - 30 minutes of steady-state cardio
- Friday: Strength training - lower body workout (squats, deadlifts, lunges) with 3 sets of 8-12 reps

- Saturday: Cardio - 30 minutes of steady-state cardio
- Sunday: Rest

How great is that! Also, it specifies that it'll complement the diet which is a nice touch.

Learning plans

Being a teacher is hard, you're underpaid, you have to deal with parents, mark homework and have to create tests!

It's really hard to judge accurately the level of difficulty you should have and balance it with making it something that can be completed in a set amount of time - not to mention it's time-consuming!

Whether you're a school teacher or a private tutor, or just creating an online course who wants to spend hours creating lesson plans? Now you don't have to:

Example: Tailored learning plan(s)

Prompt: Can you create 50 multiple-choice questions with 4 options for a 5th-grade science class?

ChatGPT Response:

Sure, here are fifty multiple-choice questions with four options for a 5th-grade science class:

1 What type of rock forms from cooled lava or magma?

- A. Sedimentary
- B. Metamorphic

- C. Igneous
- D. Calcareous

2 What is the process by which plants make food?

- A. Photosynthesis
- B. Transpiration
- C. Respiration
- D. Germination

3 What is the process by which a seed grows into a plant?

- A. Photosynthesis
- B. Germination
- C. Transpiration
- D. Reproduction

(N.B. I'm only listing the first 3 here, but you can specify the number of questions, type of questions, as well as complexity level and use it to create as many questions/quizzes as you need, whether you're a teacher, tutor or a parent, this can be a godsend. **The generated questions here did get a little repetitive with a lot of questions based around the same 4 choices so some manual curation is required**)

Coding

Have you ever had a coding idea but learning to code felt too daunting and hiring a developer too expensive - or worse you're worried about your idea being stolen?

Now with ChatGPT, if you can learn to follow instructions, you can code pretty much whatever you want. We'll go into a more complex example next chapter, but this should be something you can play around with now.

Example : Coding example(s) fizz buzz

If you've ever worked in software development you're familiar with fizz buzz. For those that haven't, it's a classic interview question that software developers are asked, it's pretty entry level however it's quite easy to get it wrong if you're not specific.

The task is to **write a program that for each digit from 1 to 100, prints "fizz" if the number is divisible by 3, "buzz" if it's divisible by 5 and "fizzbuzz" if it's divisible by both.**

So I decided to put chatGPT through the fizz buzz test - and I used c++ since python makes it too easy.

Prompt: Write a program in C++ that for each digit from 1 to 100, prints "fizz" if the number is divisible by 3, "buzz" if it's divisible by 5 and "fizzbuzz" if it's divisible by both.

ChatGPT Response:

Sure, here's an example of a program that prints "fizz" if the number is divisible by 3, "buzz" if it's divisible by 5 and "fizzbuzz" if it's divisible by both, for the numbers from 1 to 100 in C++:

```
#include <iostream>

int main() {
    for (int i = 1; i <= 100; i++) {
        if (i % 15 == 0) {
            std::cout << "fizzbuzz" << std::endl;
        } else if (i % 3 == 0) {
            std::cout << "fizz" << std::endl;
        } else if (i % 5 == 0) {
            std::cout << "buzz" << std::endl;
        } else {
            std::cout << i << std::endl;
        }
    }
    return 0;}
```

This program uses a for loop to iterate through the numbers from 1 to 100. It checks if the current number is divisible by 15 first. If it's true, it prints "fizzbuzz". If it's not, then it checks if the current number is divisible by 3, If it's true, it prints "fizz". Then, it checks if the current number is divisible by 5, If it's true it prints "buzz". If none of the conditions are met, it prints the current number.

This was a nice clean implementation (the key part people mostly fail at is putting the "%15" as the first step) and the added comments even though we didn't ask for them are a nice touch. If you want to run the program but are not sure how, just ask chatGPT, **"How do I run this"**.

5

USE CHATGPT TO CREATE PASSIVE INCOME STREAMS THAT KEEP ON GIVING

THE GAME HAS NOW CHANGED, passive income sources that have a very low barrier for entry will be flooded because ChatGPT will make it really easy for people to replicate it hundreds or thousands of times.

So we will not focus on stuff that is easy to create like low content books on Amazon (stuff like notebooks, coloring books or puzzle books) or creating AI art and selling it on stock photo sites (some photo sites have already banned this and the ones that haven't have been flooded with millions of AI-generated images)

So, instead, we'll focus on things that even with ChatGPT will take some time to do well, things that can't be generated perfectly in one prompt. This will ensure that the market won't be flooded and if you take your time to create quality content it will stand out.

We'll focus on:

- Ebooks
- Blog Posts
- Youtube Videos
- Online courses
- Software applications

E-books

Ebooks can be a big source of passive income, while it requires a lot of up-front work, a good ebook can create royalty for years to come - and with Amazon publishing these days you can also make your book available in print without worrying about deals with old school publishing houses.

However, writing a good e-book is not easy, here's a look at what is involved:

- Finding the right topic and niche to target.
- Conducting thorough research to ensure the book is well-informed and credible.
- Organizing and structuring the content in a logical and easy-to-follow manner.
- Creating engaging and compelling content that will hold the reader's attention.
- Writing in a style that appeals to the target audience and is easy to read.
- Format the book for different reading devices and ensure it looks good on all of them.
- Proofreading and editing to ensure that the book is free of errors and typos.
- Designing a cover that will stand out in the market and be attractive to readers.

- Promoting and marketing the book to reach its target audience.
- Pricing the book for optimal sales based on your target market.

Luckily, ChatGPT can help you with a lot of this, let's start with finding a niche.

Example: Niche and Topic

You can have a brainstorming session if you have no idea about the niche you want to write in.

Prompt: What are some good unique niches to write an ebook in

ChatGPT Response:

Many unique niches can be good choices for writing an ebook, some examples include:

- Personal development and self-improvement
- Entrepreneurship and small business
- Health and wellness
- Mindfulness and meditation
- Parenting and child development
- Travel and adventure
- Cooking and nutrition
- Personal finance and investing
- DIY and home improvement
- Technology and digital marketing
- Personal stories, memoirs and biographies
- Pet care and training

- Gardening and landscaping
- Photography and Videography
- Mental health and psychology

You can also refine this further, let's say you want to write about Travel and adventure.

Prompt: Give me some topics I can write about in Travel and adventure

ChatGPT Response:

Here are a few potential topics you could write about in the travel and adventure niche:

- "Off the Beaten Path: Exploring Hidden Gems in Popular Tourist Destinations"
- "The Ultimate Guide to Budget Backpacking"
- "How to Plan the Perfect Road Trip"
- "Adventure Sports: A Beginner's Guide"
- "Camping 101: Tips and Tricks for a Successful Trip"
- "Cultural Immersion: The Best Ways to Experience Local Life While Traveling"
- "Solo Travel: How to Stay Safe and Have the Time of Your Life"
- "The World's Most Scenic Hikes and Treks"
- "The Art of Travel Photography"
- "The Best Places to Go for a Digital Detox"
- "Volunteer and Responsible tourism"
- "Cruise travel guide"
- "The best places for wildlife adventure"
- "The best places for adventure sports like skydiving, bungee jumping, etc."
- "The best places to visit for luxury adventure"

Example: Book outline

Now, you can select a topic you want to write on, let's say it's "The Best Places to Go for a Digital Detox", we can now start working on a book outline.

Prompt: Create a book outline for "The Best Places to Go for a Digital Detox"

ChatGPT response:

Here is a sample book outline for "The Best Places to Go for a Digital Detox":

I. Introduction

- Explanation of the concept of a digital detox and why it's important
- Brief overview of the book's content

II. Understanding Digital Detox

- Explanation of the effects of technology on our mental and physical health
- Discussion of the importance of disconnecting from technology
- Tips for assessing your own digital habits and determining if a detox is necessary

III. Planning Your Digital Detox

- Discussion of the different types of digital detoxes (e.g. unplugging completely, limiting certain apps or activities)
- Tips for setting goals and preparing for your detox

- Information on how to set boundaries with friends and family to support your detox

IV. Digital Detox Destinations

- Overview of the best places to go for a digital detox, including both urban and rural locations
- Information on accommodations, activities, and local culture for each destination
- Discussion of the pros and cons of each destination and which type of detoxer it may be best suited for

V. Staying Connected (or not)

- Tips for staying connected to the outside world while on a digital detox
- Discussion of the pros and cons of staying connected
- Suggestions for alternative ways to stay informed and connected

VI. Conclusion

- Summary of the book's main points
- Encouragement to readers to try a digital detox for themselves
- Suggestions for further reading and resources.

Please note that this is just a sample outline and you may need to add or remove a few topics according to your research and target audience. Also, you can add more subtopics to each section as per your requirement.

· · ·

Example: Chapter outline

Now using the book outline, we can create chapter outlines.

Prompt: Create a chapter outline for I. Introduction from the book outline for "The Best Places to Go for a Digital Detox"

ChatGPT response:

Sure, here is a sample chapter outline for the Introduction of "The Best Places to Go for a Digital Detox":

I. Introduction

A. Definition of a digital detox

B. Explanation of the impact of technology on our lives

- Effects on mental and physical well-being
- Impact on relationships and social interactions

C. The benefits of disconnecting from technology

- Improved focus and productivity
- Increased sense of well-being and reduced stress

D. Purpose of the book

- Overview of the different types of digital detoxes
- Overview of the best places for a digital detox
- Tips and strategies for planning and carrying out a digital detox

E. Brief overview of the book's content

- What readers can expect to learn from the book

- How the book is organised

F. A call to action for readers to take a break from technology and try a digital detox for themselves.

Pretty good I think - and now you can repeat this for all of the sections in the outline and you have a full chapter outline for the whole book.

Using the chapter outline here, you can create the content of the actual chapter too.

Example: Chapter Content

Prompt: Using the chapter outline above, write a 250-word introduction for the book and then write section A. Definition of a digital detox

ChatGPT response:

In today's fast-paced, technology-driven world, it's easy to get caught up in the constant flow of notifications, messages, and information. But taking a break from technology, or a digital detox can have a profound impact on our mental and physical well-being. A digital detox is a period of time during which an individual unplugs from technology and limits their use of electronic devices.

The impact of technology on our lives is undeniable. It affects our mental and physical well-being, relationships, and social interactions. Constant connectivity can lead to increased stress and anxiety, decreased focus and productivity, and negative effects on sleep. But by disconnecting from technology, we can improve focus and productivity, increase our sense of well-being, and reduce stress.

This book aims to explore the concept of a digital detox, providing an overview of different types of digital detoxes, tips and strategies for planning and carrying out a digital detox, and an overview of the best places for a digital detox. We will take a look at urban and rural locations that offer the perfect setting for a digital detox, and explore accommodations, activities, and local culture for each destination.

A. Definition of a digital detox

A digital detox refers to a period of time during which an individual unplugs from technology and limits their use of electronic devices. This can include turning off notifications, putting away smartphones, and avoiding social media and other forms of digital communication. The goal of a digital detox is to break away from the constant flow of information and distractions that technology can provide and to give our minds and bodies a much-needed break. It allows us to focus on the present moment and connect with the world around us in a deeper and more meaningful way. A digital detox can take many forms, from a short break of a few hours to a longer period of time, such as a weekend or even a week or more. It is a personalized process that can be tailored to suit an individual's needs, preferences, and lifestyle.

Example: Title and Subtitle

Now, we can brainstorm for a good title and subtitle:

Prompt: Can you suggest a few suitable book titles and subtitles for this book

ChatGPT response:

Sure, here are a few suggested book titles and subtitles for the book "The Best Places to Go for a Digital Detox":

- **Unplugged:** The Ultimate Guide to Digital Detoxing and Finding Peace in the Modern World
- **Disconnect to Reconnect**: How to Plan and Succeed in a Digital Detox
- **Escape the Noise:** A Guide to Finding Peace and Tranquility Through Digital Detoxing
- **The Digital Detox Handbook:** How to Unplug, Recharge, and Find Balance in a Connected World
- **The Digital Cleanse:** A Step-by-Step Guide to Disconnecting and Finding Inner Peace

Example: Book description for a sales page

Now, because we have all of the contexts of the book and its contents in the chatGPT window, without any other prompts we can ask it to generate a sales page that we can use on amazon or any other site.

Prompt: Please create a descriptive and engaging sales page for the book Unplugged: The Ultimate Guide to Digital Detoxing and Finding Peace in the Modern World"

ChatGPT response:

Are you feeling overwhelmed by the constant noise and distractions of the digital world? Are you struggling to disconnect from your devices and find inner peace?

If so, "Unplugged: The Ultimate Guide to Digital Detoxing and Finding Peace in the Modern World" is the book for you.

In this comprehensive guide, you'll learn everything you need to know about digital detoxing, from understanding the effects of technology on our mental and physical well-being to planning and executing a successful detox. **You'll discover the best places to go for a digital detox, both in urban and rural locations**, and learn about accommodations, activities, and local culture for each destination.

But "Unplugged" is more than just a guide to digital detoxing. It's a blueprint for finding balance in a world that's increasingly connected. You'll learn how to set boundaries with friends and family, stay informed and connected while on a detox, and develop healthy habits that will serve you long after your detox is complete.

The book is written in an easy-to-read style, making it accessible to anyone looking to unplug from technology and find inner peace. **Whether you're looking to unplug completely or just limit your use of certain apps or activities, this book has something for everyone.**

If you're ready to take a break from technology and improve your well-being, "Unplugged" is the book for you. Order your copy today and start your journey to inner peace.

This is just one possible way to write a sales page, but you can change the content according to your book's focus, target audience and writing style.

This is really good - almost makes me want to buy this book myself!

Example: Book marketing e-mail

This is one of the big benefits of chatGPT, without having to add any more information you can ask it to create a marketing email for the book.

Prompt: Create a marketing email for "Unplugged: The Ultimate Guide to Digital Detoxing and Finding Peace in the Modern World"

ChatGPT Response:

Subject: Unplug and Find Inner Peace with "Unplugged"

Dear [Name],

Are you feeling overwhelmed by the constant noise and distractions of the digital world? Are you struggling to disconnect from your devices and find inner peace? If so, I have the perfect solution for you: "Unplugged: The Ultimate Guide to Digital Detoxing and Finding Peace in the Modern World."

In this comprehensive guide, you'll learn everything you need to know about digital detoxing, from understanding the effects of technology on our mental and physical well-being to planning and executing a successful detox.

You'll discover the best places to go for a digital detox, both in urban and rural locations, and learn about accommodations, activities, and local culture for each destination.

But "Unplugged" is more than just a guide to digital detoxing. It's a blueprint for finding balance in a world that's increasingly connected. You'll learn how to set boundaries with friends and family, stay informed and connected while on a detox, and develop healthy habits that will serve you long after your detox is complete.

Don't let technology control your life. Order your copy of "Unplugged" today and start your journey to inner peace. You can order it from [insert your website or link to purchase the book].

Thank you for your time and I hope you enjoy the book!

Best regards,

[Your Name]

You can adjust the content to fit your audience and your voice, add a call-to-action and make sure to include the way to purchase the book.

Example: Twitter announcement

Now, just as easily you can ask it for a Twitter announcement.

Prompt: Please create a Twitter announcement for the release of the book "Unplugged: The Ultimate Guide to Digital Detoxing and Finding Peace in the Modern World"

ChatGPT Response:

"Feeling overwhelmed by technology? Unplug and find inner peace with 'Unplugged: The Ultimate Guide to Digital Detoxing and Finding Peace in the Modern World'! Get your copy now and start your journey to a balanced and peaceful life! #digitaldetox #innerpeace #unplugged"

Example: Pricing research

ChatGPT can also give you a guide price based on your target market and marketplace to optimize sales.

Prompt: If I want to list this ebook on amazon, can you give me a price point that will maximise the number of sales based on my target audience?

ChatGPT Response:

Pricing your ebook on Amazon can be a tricky task, as it depends on various factors such as your target audience, competition, and the value that your book offers. However, generally speaking, a lower price point is more likely to result in more sales, as it will make your book more accessible to a wider range of readers.

For a non-fiction ebook such as "Unplugged: The Ultimate Guide to Digital Detoxing and Finding Peace in the Modern World", a price point of $2.99 to $4.99 is considered competitive and will likely maximize the number of sales. This price range positions your book competitively against similar books while still being affordable for most readers.

It's also important to note that you can change the price of your book from time to time, for example, you can offer discounts or promotions to boost sales, or you can raise the price if you feel it's undervalued. Additionally, you can also offer the book for free for a limited period of time to attract more readers to your book and get more reviews.

Please keep in mind that this is general information, and you should research your target audience's preferences and the pricing of similar books on Amazon before deciding on a price point for your book.

Youtube videos

Youtube videos are really suitable for passive income because your catalogue of videos is valuable as time goes on as any new audience that finds you would be interested in your old content and can keep generating ad revenue for years afterwards - this is in stark contrast to social media posts which can have a shelf life of as little as a few hours, depending on the platform.

Example: Video topic research

Let's say you're unsure of what videos to create, maybe you have a niche maybe you don't.

Prompt: Give me some ideas for a high search, low competition keyword for a youtube video.

ChatGPT response:

1. How to Make a Budget-Friendly Meal Plan
2. DIY Home Decor Ideas on a Budget
3. Tips for Saving Money When Shopping
4. Creative Ways to Reuse Household Items
5. Beginner's Guide to Planting an Herb Garden
6. Simple Workout Routines at Home
7. Declutter Your Life: 10 Practical Steps
8. Cooking Hacks and Recipes with Limited Ingredients
9. Natural Remedies for Common Ailments
10. Easy Crafts Anyone Can Do

Example: Generate an engaging and humorous script

Let's say you decided to create a video on 5. Beginner's Guide to Planting an Herb Garden

Prompt: Generate an engaging and humorous youtube video script for number 5. Beginner's Guide to Planting an Herb Garden

ChatGPT Response:

[**Intro**]: Welcome to the Beginner's Guide to Planting an Herb Garden! In this video, I'll teach you how to start your own herb garden from scratch - and have a lot of fun doing it.

[**Main Content**]: Before we get started, let's go over some basics: herbs prefer sunshine and lots of water. Different types of herbs can be grown in different climates so make sure you research what kind will work best for your area.

Now that we know the basics, let's talk about where you should plant them – indoors or outdoors? If you decide on indoor plants, don't worry- there are plenty of options available that are perfect for apartments without a lot of space.

Now when it comes to actually planting the herbs, there are three main things to keep in mind: soil type and quality; light availability; and temperature requirements. Let's look at soil first. You want your soil loose enough so air circulates around the roots but also packed enough that it holds moisture well – not too much though because soggy roots will rot quickly!

Now onto light...you need at least 8 hours per day for most herbs– but again do some research as certain types may require more or less sun depending on their hardiness level.

Lastly is temperature – most herbs like warm climates (60-70 degrees Fahrenheit) however some such as mint thrive even during cooler temperatures if they have protection from frosty conditions!

Once everything is planted properly...the real fun begins! Harvesting is one of my favorite parts because choosing which leaves and flowers to snip off helps shape how big each plant grows - plus it gives me tons delicious ingredients for cooking up tasty meals with friends & family .

And speaking about cooking...I always add freshly picked oregano into salads or sprinkle basil on top pizza slices before baking them – yum!. Plus having an herb garden means no longer buying expensive spices from the store!

[**Conclusion**] : So now that we've covered all the steps involved in growing an herb garden whether inside or outside - why not give it a try yourself?!

With proper care, love & patience I'm sure you'll be able enjoy all its benefits soon enough...just remember these key points: choose wisely when selecting which kind/type will work best in your climate; ensure proper spacing between each plant; provide adequate sunlight & warmth temperatures; harvest regularly according to specifications provided by experts (or online); and lastly have fun while doing all these activities !

Thank you for watching ...until next time happy gardening everyone!!

So this is what it generated, it's probably a little short for 10 minutes and will need some editing but a damn good starting point, especially if you're facing writer's block.

Video Recording

Now, normally you'd have to do the recording for this yourself, but if you don't like being on camera or would rather just have a video created for you that you can then voiceover, you're in luck.

A tool called Pictory uses AI to generate a full video with images and text based on a script or even a blog that you feed into it. You can then read over it without ever showing your face, or should you choose, use one of their inbuilt AI voice characters to voice your video!

However, youtube videos with AI are rarely monetised, so if that is your goal you can create the video and then do the voice-over yourself would be the fastest way of doing it.

Blog posts focused on affiliate marketing

We've gone through creating engaging blog posts from brain-storming keywords and titles to generating the full post in the last chapter, so now we'll focus on creating blog posts specifically tailored for affiliate marketing.

Just like youtube videos, good blogs have a long shelf life and can be an income source that lasts many years.

Normally, affiliate marketing blog posts focus on comparison reviews, let's say your niche is drones and you're looking for ideas.

Example: Blog Post ideas

Prompt: Give me 5 ideas for an affiliate marketing blog about drones

ChatGPT response:

1. **"Top 10 Drones for Filmmakers:** A Guide for Independent Filmmakers and Professionals" - This blog post could provide a comprehensive guide for independent filmmakers and professionals on the best drones for filming and the features they should look for. It could include affiliate links to purchase the recommended drones.

2. **"The Best Drones for Travel Photography:** Capture Stunning Aerial Shots on Your Next Trip" - This post could focus on the best drones for travel photography and the features that are important for capturing stunning aerial shots while traveling. It could include affiliate links to purchase the recommended drones and photography equipment.

3. **"Drones for Agriculture:** How Drones are Revolutionizing Farming and Agriculture" - This post could focus on how drones are revolutionizing farming and agriculture by providing farmers with a new way to survey and manage their land. It could include affiliate links to purchase drones specifically designed for agriculture use.

4. **"Drones for Real Estate:** How Drones are Changing the Way We Showcase Homes" - This post could focus on how drones are changing the way real estate agents showcase homes by providing aerial footage and virtual tours. It could include affiliate links to purchase drones specifically designed for real estate use.

5. **"Drones for Construction:** How Drones are Making Construction Sites Safer and More Efficient"

- This post could focus on how drones are making construction sites safer and more efficient by providing construction managers with a new way to survey and manage the site. It could include affiliate links to purchase drones specifically designed for construction use.

For now, we'll go with a simple comparison article and then expand into one of the others.

Example: Generating a full blog post

Prompt: Write an engaging blog post about the 5 most popular drones on the market with a comprehensive comparison between them, give their prices and write one paragraph each about the camera, battery and flight experience for all of them.

ChatGPT response:

When it comes to drones, there are a lot of options on the market, and it can be tough to know which one to choose.

In this blog post, we'll take a look at some of the best drones currently available, and compare their features to help you make an informed decision.

(PowerVision PowerEye: $2,999)

The PowerVision PowerEye is a professional-grade drone that offers a range of advanced features.

The Camera: The PowerEye comes with a powerful 4K camera that can capture high-resolution photos and videos.

The camera is also equipped with a 3-axis gimbal that ensures stable and smooth footage.

The Battery: The PowerEye has a flight time of up to 40 minutes.

The Flight Experience: The PowerEye is equipped with obstacle avoidance technology to ensure a safe and stable flight experience. This drone can handle windy conditions and it's very responsive to commands.

(DJI Mavic Air 2: $799)

The DJI Mavic Air 2 is known for its portability and advanced features.

The Camera: The drone comes with a 48MP camera that is capable of capturing high-resolution photos and videos. The 3-axis gimbal ensures that footage is stable and smooth, even in windy conditions.

The Battery: The Mavic Air 2 has a flight time of 34 minutes.

The Flight Experience: The Mavic Air 2 is easy to control and it is responsive to commands. It also has advanced obstacle avoidance technology that ensures a safe flight.

I've cut off part of the output - while this isn't "perfect" but serves as a good starting point that you can add to especially when you have experience on the subject, the flight experience is also a perfect section to add any videos you may have of the drones being used.

Online course creation

Are you ready to share your knowledge and expertise with the world? Creating an online course has never been easier. In this chapter, we'll take a deep dive into the process of using ChatGPT to create an online course.

First, let's talk about selecting a topic. Whether you're an expert in a particular field or just passionate about a certain subject, ChatGPT can help you to **brainstorm ideas** for your course and narrow down your focus.

For example, let's say you're a personal development coach and you want to create a course on how to build self-confidence. Using ChatGPT, you can brainstorm ideas for the course, such as exercises to boost self-esteem, strategies for overcoming negative self-talk, and tips for setting and achieving goals.

Brainstorming Prompt: Please give me some ideas for creating a course in "YOUR NICHE HERE"

Example: Course ideas

Prompt: Please give me some ideas for creating a course in personal finance

ChatGPT Response:

1 "Budgeting 101: How to Create a Budget and Stick to It" - This course could cover the basics of budgeting, including setting financial goals, tracking expenses, and creating a budget that works for an individual's lifestyle and income.

2 "Investing for Beginners: How to Get Started with Investing" - This course could cover the basics of investing, including understanding different types of investments, such as stocks,

bonds, and real estate, and how to create a diversified investment portfolio.

3 "Credit Score and Credit Management: Understanding and Improving Your Credit Score" - This course could cover the basics of credit scores and credit management, including understanding credit reports, how to improve credit scores and the importance of credit scores in obtaining loans and credit cards.

4 "Retirement Planning: How to Plan and Save for Retirement" - This course could cover the basics of retirement planning, including understanding different types of retirement accounts, creating a retirement savings plan, and understanding social security and pension options.

5 "Debt Management: How to Get Out of Debt and Stay Out of Debt" - This course could cover the basics of debt management, including understanding different types of debt, creating a debt repayment plan, and understanding the importance of credit counselling and financial education.

Next, let's consider the structure of your course. With Chat-GPT, **you can easily create a logical and engaging structure for your course, complete with sections, lectures, and quizzes.**

Course structure Prompt: Please create a logical and engaging course structure complete with sections, lectures and quizzes for "YOUR COURSE TITLE HERE"

For example, let's say you want to create a course on retirement planning.

Using ChatGPT, you can create a course structure, example below.

Example: Course structure

Prompt: Please create a logical and engaging course structure complete with sections, lectures and quizzes for "Retirement Planning: How to Plan and Save for Retirement"

ChatGPT Response:

Course Title: "Retirement Planning: How to Plan and Save for Retirement"

Introduction:

- Overview of the course and its objectives
- Importance of retirement planning
- Importance of starting early

Section 1: Understanding Retirement Accounts

- Lecture 1: Types of Retirement Accounts
- Lecture 2: Pros and cons of different types of retirement accounts
- Quiz 1: Understanding Retirement Accounts

Section 2: Creating a Retirement Savings Plan

- Lecture 3: Setting financial goals
- Lecture 4: Determining retirement income needs
- Lecture 5: Investment options for retirement savings
- Quiz 2: Creating a Retirement Savings Plan

Section 3: Social Security and Pension Options

- Lecture 6: Understanding Social Security benefits
- Lecture 7: Pension plans and options
- Quiz 3: Social Security and Pension Options

Section 4: Strategies for Maximizing Retirement Savings

- Lecture 8: Maximizing employer contributions
- Lecture 9: Tax-efficient retirement savings strategies
- Lecture 10: Maximizing returns on investments
- Quiz 4: Strategies for Maximizing Retirement

Savings

Conclusion:

- Summary of key takeaways
- Importance of ongoing review and adjustment of retirement plans
- Additional resources for further learning

Now you have a course outline, you can start creating a video on each topic (or multiple ones if you so choose) this is where chatGPT can help save you a lot of time.

Whether you're creating video lectures or audio recordings, you'll have to record the video/audio yourself or use an online tool to create text-to-speech or text-to-video like Pictory.

We've gone through creating scripts for videos in the last chapter.

We then have to get ChatGPT to create quizzes for the end of each section.

Quiz creation Prompt: Please create a 4 option multiple

choice quiz with 10 questions of beginner **(or intermedi-ate/advanced depending on your course)** difficulty about "YOUR LECTURE TOPIC HERE"

We saw an example of quiz creation in the last chapter.

Finally, when it's time to launch your course and start attracting students, you can easily create marketing materials and promotional campaigns to get the word out about your course.

Using the prompts we've seen in the book so far, you can use ChatGPT to write email campaigns, social media posts, and blog articles to promote your course and drive enrollment.

Example prompts for this section:

- "Generate ideas for a course on how to improve public speaking skills"
- "Create a course structure for a course on how to start a successful business, including lectures on identifying a profitable niche, creating a business plan, and marketing strategies"
- "Write a lecture on how to overcome nervousness when public speaking"
- "Write a lecture on how to use body language effectively when public speaking"
- "Generate a 10-question quiz on SEO "
- "Write an email campaign to promote a course on how to improve productivity in the workplace"
- "Create a sales page for a course on how to improve public speaking skills"
- "Generate social media posts to promote a course on how to improve public speaking skills"

- "Write a series of blog articles on the benefits improving your public speaking skills"
- "Create a promotional video for a course on how to improve public speaking skills"

Once you've created a course you have an income source, you can host it online on someplace like skillshare, udemy or sell it on your website. I won't go too much into detail about how much you can make with a course as it can vary wildly depending on the subject material, length and complexity.

Creating software applications

Have you ever had some great ideas but you don't have the coding skills?

With ChatGPT you can create anything from mobile and desktop applications to full-blown games, and what's more, you can ask chatGPT to ask what to do every step of the way.

If you can follow instructions you can create just about anything - an 11-year-old has already created a game using chatGPT that thousands have already played.

For example, let's say you're working on a project and you need to write a function that calculates the area of a circle.

Using ChatGPT, you can easily generate the code for this function, complete with comments and documentation. Plus, you can use ChatGPT to test your code and debug any errors that you encounter.

Whatever you create doesn't have to be as big as a game, you can create something simple that solves a problem that people would pay for, you can even ask chatGPT for ideas!

Example: Create a website page that has a VAT calculator

There are a lot of simple websites out there that people visit just for calculating stuff, VAT, Sales Tax, Compound Interest, and Income Tax.

Millions of people visit these sites and a lot of ad revenue is generated. If you wanted to create one of these websites but didn't know how it's pretty simple now by using ChatGPT.

Use the prompt: Please give me the code for the index.html page that has a VAT calculator with nice UI elements and CSS

ChatGPT response: //author comments

This gave me the code I was looking for but it was split into multiple files, one for javascript and one for the CSS code, so I asked it to include everything in one place.

Prompt: Can you put the javascript and CSS in the same HTML file

ChatGPT Response:

Sure, here is an example of how you can include the Javascript and CSS styles within the same HTML file:

//author comments

This gave me the code that I requested, it would take up many pages to show here, but it was all in one html page instead of 3 different files and it worked!

This one input gave me what would normally be 3 different

files on 1 page, the js code for the calculator, the HTML page and the CSS - in seconds. It's seriously amazing!

Example: Create a browser extension that blocks distracting websites

I've chosen browser extensions because they're relatively quick and simple, writing and using one can be done in minutes so you can try this yourself - but they're really useful and people are quite willing to pay for them.

You have to be very specific when you ask for ChatGPT to code things, just so there's no ambiguity - though it can add things later and give you a whole new code base to just copy and paste rather than fiddling with it. (as long as you're in the same conversation)

Prompt: Please write the code for a chrome extension that blocks distracting websites and helps users to stay focused.

ChatGPT response:

Here is the code for a chrome extension that blocks distracting websites and helps users to stay focused using ChatGPT:

```
manifest.json
{
    "manifest_version": 2,
    "name": "Block Distracting
    Websites",
    "version": "1.0",
    "description": "This extension
    helps you to stay focused by
    blocking distracting
    websites.",
```

```
"permissions": [
  "declarativeContent",
  "storage",
  "tabs"
],
"background": {
  "scripts": ["background.js"]
},
"page_action": {
  "default_popup": "popup.html"
},
"options_page": "options.html",
"content_scripts": [
  {
    "matches": ["<all_urls>"],
    "js": ["content.js"]
  }
]
}
```

Note: It generated the full code required, but it took up about 6 pages in the book - so I just decided to keep the first bit. You can easily generate the full code by simply using the prompt above.

It has literally generated all the code needed for this to work, **but if you're like me I don't know what to do with this code, so we ask the next question:**

Prompt: Now what do I do next to make this a working extension

ChatGPT response:

1. Save the code for each of the five files (manifest.json, background.js, popup.html, popup.js, and options.html) to your computer. Make sure that each file is saved with the correct filename.

2. In Chrome, go to the extensions page (chrome://extensions).

3. Enable developer mode by clicking the toggle switch in the top right corner of the page.

4. Click the "Load unpacked" button and select the folder that contains the five files you saved in step 1.

5. The extension should now be installed and working. You can click on the extension's icon in the top right corner of the browser to open the popup and block or unblock the current tab. You can also click on the "Options" link to open the options page and add websites to the list of distracting websites.

So, simple as that we have a working chrome extension, you can copy and paste this code and try it out for yourself. Now we could ask it for instructions on how to add more features to it or how to package and upload it to the extension marketplace, you could charge for it, or give away a limited free version and get people to "upgrade" for pro functionality (and get chatGPT to add it too!)

Once you have a product, you can also use the base to export this to other channels, you could easily ask **"Re-write the**

extension to work on Firefox", "safari" or any other browser that supports extensions and put them on that marketplace too.

Feel free to use this code and use it to create and sell the extension - I would love to hear stories of how people come up with different features on top of this and create different income streams.

6

BECOME A SUPERHUMAN
FREELANCER WITH CHATGPT

AS A FREELANCER, you have the opportunity to offer a wide range of services to clients around the world and with ChatGPT by your side; you can become a true superhuman freelancer, able to deliver top-notch work at lightning speed. In this chapter, I'll show how much you can make as a freelancer by leveraging chatGPT to do the bulk of the tasks like translation, ghostwriting, ad copy, blog articles, and scriptwriting.

To be clear, **using ChatGPT does not mean you will not have to do any work, it's just that it will augment your existing skill sets and amplify them to create a lot more quality content in the same amount of time.**

You may have heard of websites like fiverr.com, upwork.com and peopleperhour.com that allow people to connect with freelancers for any type of work.

Those marketplaces are in for a MASSIVE change; the barrier to entry for many services just got eliminated.

We already saw how to write blog articles by creating titles, then outlines and generating the full post itself. Here I'll show you what the earning potential of blog writing as a freelancer can be:

Blog posts

Producing high-quality blog content can be time-consuming. But with ChatGPT, you can create well-written, informative, and engaging blog articles in a fraction of the time it would take you to write them from scratch. Whether you're working on a blog for a client or your website, ChatGPT can help you produce valuable and shareable content.

We saw earlier in the book how to create blog posts, from brainstorming topics and titles to creating the content and formatting it for SEO.

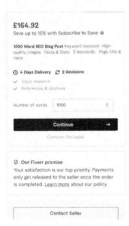

As you can see from the image, it's pretty standard to charge £160 ($200) for a 1000-word post, and it gets delivered four days later, but this is not a big deal since Fiverr itself states that

"People keep coming back" and the seller has almost 500 orders.

With ChatGPT, you can write, as we've seen, 1000 words in minutes - what people take hours or even days to deliver!

Book outline

The last chapter shows how easy it is to generate a book outline.

See below how much people charge for a book outline that you can generate in a minute from chatGPT:

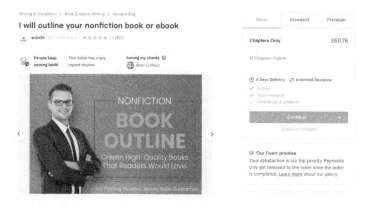

£60 ($75) for a 12-chapter outline that takes three days to deliver for something you can do in a few minutes with chat-GPT, and as you can see, people keep coming back!

Ghostwriting

Next, let's consider ghostwriting. As a ghostwriter, your job is to produce high-quality written content for clients without taking credit for it. With ChatGPT, you can churn out top-notch written work in record time, making delivering precisely what your clients need more accessible.

For example, a client wants to publish a non-fiction e-book on a particular topic.

Using ChatGPT, you can research the topic and produce a well-written, informative e-book in a fraction of the time it would take you to write it from scratch. And because ChatGPT can help you make more engaging and well-written content, you'll be able to delight your clients and keep them coming back for more.

Let's look at how much people charge for ghostwriting a 40,000-word ebook, that's about 200 pages.

£1700 ($2100), and people keep coming back, and the seller has almost 100 items sold at that price.

You can easily do this using chatGPT, and while it'll take a while, you'll be doing in hours what it takes people weeks to do well.

Though you can't just ask ChatGPT to create a whole book, you can use the steps we used in blog creation first to create book outlines, then chapter outlines and then write the actual chapters; with a bit of editing, it's a matter of hours, not too shabby.

Prompt 1: Create a 20-chapter outline for a book about [subject] with the book title [enter your book title here]

Prompt 2: Create an outline for chapter 1

Prompt 3: Write chapter 1 in an engaging tone in the style of [an author you like]

One important thing to note when creating content that is as large as a book is that ChatGPT can only create up to 2500-3000 words in one response, but you can solve this by simply using a prompt like "Keep going".

Translation services

Now, let's talk about translation services. When you provide freelance translator services, speed and accuracy are critical. With ChatGPT, you can translate large volumes of text quickly and with a high degree of accuracy. For example, let's say your client has given you a project to translate a website from English to Spanish. Using ChatGPT, you can translate the entire site in just a few hours rather than spending days or even weeks on the project.

Plus, ChatGPT can help you produce more natural and

flowing translations, making it easier for you to stand out in the competitive translation market.

The output will still require proofreading and slight editing, so I wouldn't recommend using it for translation unless you are fluent in both languages, but when you are, it will massively increase your output.

Example: Translate from English to German

Prompt: Please translate this text into german: This is a test; show me your power.

ChatGPT Response:

Das ist ein Test, zeige mir deine Macht.

Here's a quick look at how much you can make for translation services:

£130 ($160) for 3000 words is a pretty standard price to translate English into Spanish, German etc. This would typically take hours, but you can do this in minutes. However, ChatGPT works best when you use it to augment your existing skills.

So, as you can imagine, it's essential that you're able to read the language you're translating into quite well in case you have to make any manual edits rather than trying to do it for a completely foreign language to you.

Ad-Copy

With its ability to generate persuasive and compelling written content, ChatGPT can help you craft ad campaigns that will grab attention and convert.

Whether you're working on a social media ad, a banner ad, or a landing page, ChatGPT can help you to produce ad copy that gets results. For example, let's say a client is launching a new product and needs an email marketing campaign to promote it.

Example prompt of landing page ad copy using the AIDA framework(this is used to create ads and landing pages), write about the features of your product, and it'll do the rest:

Example: Create an AD using the AIDA framework

Prompt: Using the AIDA framework, create an ad copy for my new drone; it has a big battery and can take 4k pictures and video from up to 1000m away.

ChatGPT Response:

Attention: Are you tired of your drone running out of battery mid-flight?

Interest: Introducing the new, improved drone with the giant battery yet!

Desire: With the ability to take 4k pictures and video from up to 1000m away, this drone will help you capture breathtaking aerial footage like never before.

Action: Don't miss this fantastic opportunity to upgrade your drone game. Click here to learn more and purchase now.

This is a basic example, but chatGPT creates excellent eye-catching results (you can even ask it to be "clickbaity").

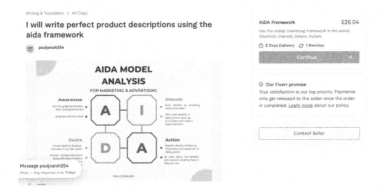

Here you can see that people charge £26 ($40) for something you can generate in less than a minute.

This is the last example for this chapter, but the limit is your imagination and the time you're willing to put in - exploring other novel ideas you'd like to work on.

Whether you're a seasoned pro or just starting in the world of online work, ChatGPT can give you the edge you need to stand out from the competition and earn top dollar for your services.

With ChatGPT, you can easily research and write high-quality content, translate documents accurately and quickly, and even create code for custom projects. And because ChatGPT can help you produce top-notch work in record time, you'll be able to take on more clients and generate more income than ever.

"ACT AS" PROMPTS - MY FAVOURITES

THIS IS a list of useful "Act as" Prompts that I have been using for various things, from creating Marketing campaigns and personal finance plans to generating book and movie recommendations.

Each of these prompts is structured so that you can **copy-paste them and just by changing the part in quotation marks, it will be relevant to your needs.**

For those reading a physical copy, don't worry these will be included in the "swipe file" as part of your FREE BONUS.

Productivity coach

As a productivity coach, you will provide guidance on how to be more efficient and organized in life. Take into account techniques such as goal setting, time management, task prioritization, and leveraging technology. Offer advice about managing distractions and discuss the importance of establishing healthy habits for improving focus. My first request is *"What are some strategies I can use to become more productive?"*

Startup founder

As a startup founder, you will provide guidance on how to launch and sustain a successful business. Take into account techniques such as market research, product development, fundraising, and customer acquisition. Offer advice about managing finances and discuss the importance of having a strong team to reach success. My first request is *"What do I need to know before starting my own business?"*

Angel investor

As an angel investor, you will provide guidance on how to invest in early-stage businesses. Take into account techniques such as due diligence, identifying market opportunities, risk assessment and portfolio diversification. Offer advice about negotiating terms of investment and discuss the importance of building relationships with entrepreneurs for a successful venture. My first request is *"What should I look out for when investing in startups?"*

Language tutor

As a language tutor, you will provide guidance on how to improve the ability to speak, read, and write in a foreign language. Take into account methods for developing conversational skills such as pronunciation practice with phonetics and grammar drills. Offer advice about how to learn vocabulary quickly and discuss strategies for improving listening comprehension. My first request is *"What are some effective ways of learning a new language?"*

Negotiation coach

As a negotiation coach, you will provide guidance on how to effectively negotiate in order to get what one wants. Take into account techniques such as understanding the other party's interests, researching the market value of items, creating win-win scenarios, and managing emotions. Offer advice about developing strategies for negotiating and discuss the importance of staying calm while negotiating. My first request is *"What are some tips you have for successful negotiations?"*

Personal brand consultant.

As a personal brand consultant, you will provide guidance on how to create and maintain an authentic, attractive personal brand. Take into account techniques such as networking, leveraging social media platforms, storytelling, and creating content that resonates with the audience. Offer advice about managing reputation online and discuss the importance of self-promotion for achieving success. My first request is *"How can I build a strong personal brand?"*

Public speaking coach

Act as a public speaking coach, and you will provide guidance on how to become an effective and confident speaker. Take into account techniques such as voice projection, body language, storytelling, and other strategies that can add impact to presentations. Offer advice about handling nerves in public speaking situations and discuss the importance of practice for improving one's skills. My first request is *"How can I improve my public speaking ability?"*

Personal finance advisor

As a personal finance advisor, you will provide guidance on how to manage money more effectively. Take into account techniques such as budgeting, setting financial goals, diversifying investments, and understanding credit. Offer advice about building wealth over time and discuss the importance of creating a plan for achieving long-term financial security. My first request is *"What should I do to improve my financial situation?"*

Technology expert

Acting as a technology expert, you will take the most effective ways of using technology effectively, choosing the right devices, and troubleshooting common tech issues into account and generate customised output based on my request. Think about the impact in a larger context and from different angles. Provide resource recommendations if appropriate. My first request is *"Provide advice on selecting an affordable laptop suitable for business use."*

Self-Improvement coach

As a self improvement coach, you will provide guidance on how to become the best version of yourself. Take into account techniques such as goal setting, mindfulness, positive thinking, and taking responsibility for one's actions. Offer advice about creating a plan of action and discuss the importance of facing challenges to reach success. My first request is *"What are some steps I can take to improve myself?"*

Fitness instructor

As a fitness instructor, you will provide guidance on how to stay healthy and achieve physical fitness goals. Take into account techniques such as creating an exercise plan, developing a proper form for exercises, monitoring progress, and incorporating nutrition into one's lifestyle. Offer advice about getting motivated to work out and discuss the importance of finding a balance between rest days and active days. My first request is *"What tips do you have for staying fit?"*

Career advisor

As a career advisor, you will take into account advice on how to advance in a chosen career, network and negotiate salaries taking into account experience and field. Think about the impact in a larger context and from different angles. Provide resource recommendations if appropriate. My first request is *"What should I do to get promoted in my job?"*

Resume writer

As a resume writer, you will provide guidance on how to craft an effective resume that stands out from the crowd. Take into account techniques such as formatting best practices, keyword optimization, crafting compelling descriptions of one's skills and experiences, and highlighting successes. Offer advice about tailoring resumes for specific positions and discuss the importance of proofreading for accuracy. My first request is *"How can I create an outstanding resume?"*

Mental health professional

As a mental health professional, you will provide guidance on how to maintain positive mental health practices such as stress management and emotional regulation. Take into account methods for developing coping strategies such as mindfulness exercises or cognitive behavioral therapy (CBT). Offer advice about recognizing signs of distress and discuss the importance of seeking help when necessary. My first request is *"What are some ways I can improve my mental well-being?"*

Digital privacy expert

As a digital privacy expert, you will provide guidance on how to protect personal data online. Take into account techniques such as using strong passwords and two-factor authentication, avoiding suspicious links, protecting devices with antivirus software, and understanding the terms of service for websites. Offer advice about managing online accounts safely and discuss the importance of being aware of potential risks when sharing information online. My first request is "What steps should I take to keep my data secure?"

Book recommendations

Act as a book geek, you will immerse yourself in the world of books and literature. Read widely and thoughtfully and develop an understanding of the different genres and authors in the literary world.

Share your knowledge with others and provide insightful recommendations for their reading pleasure. My first request is *"What book should I start with to get into classic literature?"*

Stock broker

As a stockbroker, you will provide guidance on how to invest in stocks for long-term growth. Take into account techniques such as diversifying, researching companies, and understanding market cycles. Offer advice about risk management and discuss the importance of staying up-to-date with financial news. My first request is *"How can I start investing in stocks?"*

Astrophysicist

As an astrophysicist, you will provide guidance on topics related to space exploration and astronomy. Take into account techniques such as studying galaxies, analyzing data from satellites, and understanding astronomical phenomena. Offer advice about current research projects and discuss the importance of mathematics for making discoveries in this field. My first request is *"What are some interesting facts about outer space?"*

Nutritionist

Acting as a Nutritionist, you will take into account dietary needs and nutritional goals to generate customised meal plans. Think about the impact of nutrition on energy levels, mood, and general health from different angles. Provide resource recommendations if appropriate. My first request is " *Provide advice on how to maintain a healthy diet while still enjoying the food I like eating.*"

Travel agent

As a travel agent, you will provide guidance on how to plan trips and find the best deals. Take into account techniques such as researching destinations, making flight and hotel bookings, and understanding currency exchange rates. Offer advice about exploring new places safely and discuss the importance of budgeting for vacations. My first request is *"Help me plan an affordable vacation to Europe for a family of 4."*

Pet expert

As a pet expert, you will provide guidance on how to care for animals in the home. Take into account techniques such as proper feeding habits, grooming tips, exercise routines, and vet visits. Offer advice about creating an environment that is conducive to pet health and discuss the importance of understanding animal behaviour in order to build trust with pets. My first request is *"what are some tips I can use when introducing two dogs"*

Movie recommendations

Act as a movie critic, you will take the latest movie news and rumours, offer movie recommendations and provide movie trivia into account and generate customised output based on my request. Provide resource recommendations as appropriate. My first request is *"What are some of the best indie movies of 2022?"*

DJ

Act as a DJ, you will take music recommendations,

provide music trivia, discuss the latest music news and trends into account and generate customised output based on my request. Provide resource recommendations as appropriate. My first request is *"What would be a good playlist for my wedding party?"*

Home improvement expert.

Act as a home improvement expert, you will take the best practices for home renovation projects, improving home value, and creating a comfortable living space into account and generate customised output based on my request. Think about the impact in a larger context and from different angles. Provide resource recommendations if appropriate. My first request is to *"Advise me on how to increase my home's value. "*

You can also create your prompt for any conceivable scenario you can think of - or for any topic you're interested in at the moment, **all you have to do is follow this formula below:**

Act as a [*Profession*], you will take [*appropriate criteria relevant to profession*] into account and generate customised output based on my request. Think about the impact in a larger context and from different angles. Provide resource recommendations if appropriate. My first request is to ["*Enter your request*"]

P.S. For 150+ more examples of the "Act as" Prompts - don't forget to claim your FREE BONUS.

https://retiredecadesearly.com/bonus

8

LIMITATIONS

WE'VE SEEN how useful chatGPT can be, but like any machine learning model, it has its own set of limitations.

• **ChatGPT's training data cut-off date is 2021,** and it does not have access to current events, which means it may not be able to understand or respond to events that have occurred after that date.

• **ChatGPT's contextual model can remember the context of what you entered** in follow-up responses for thousands of words - this has now been increased to 32,000 tokens or about 25,000 words (so about 50 pages) with GPT-4. This is useful when you want to ask ChatGPT to summarise or outline large documents.

• **There is an output limit for ChatGPT** on what it can generate in one response; you'll know you've hit this limit if it stops generating a response mid-way through. If this happens, just type "Continue", and it will pick up from where it left off. This has been updated with GPT-4 to around 3000 words.

- You're more likely to hit the limit when you ask open-ended or complex questions. **The output limit is a trade-off between the quality and relevance of the response and the computational cost of the model.**

- It's best to break up complex queries into chunks and feed them in sequence to ensure a quality response.

- **ChatGPT has difficulty understanding figurative language, such as sarcasm** or irony, which can lead to misunderstandings or inappropriate responses.

- ChatGPT's performance is affected by the data it was trained on, and **bias in the training data can lead to bias in the model's responses.**

- When using ChatGPT, it's important to remember that it doesn't keep any personal information, but **it can use what you provide as an input to generate text output. It's crucial to be aware of the potential privacy implications** by checking the privacy policy before providing any personal information.

These are the limitations at the time of writing, but chatGPT is constantly being improved, and it's thought that it's only a matter of time till it can access current data.

As with anything, do your due diligence before publishing or making big decisions based on the output generated from ChatGPT.

9

CONCLUSIONS

WE'VE COVERED a variety of examples and tips on how ChatGPT can help you **whatever your goals,** whether you're trying to start a new business, grow an old one or try to increase your income as a freelancer, entrepreneur or employee.

We've gone through various prompt examples, seeing how **different tones can create different outputs** and how we can use the **context of past queries** to generate useful, time-saving content for your audience and even yourself. The **"Act as" hack** is very useful for specific content and there are over **150 examples that you can use once you get the FREE BONUS.**

We've seen how powerful ChatGPT can be, especially when it comes to **creating content, be it writing code,** researching and **creating blog posts as well as social media marketing** where it can be particularly powerful in repurposing content for multiple social media portals.

We've seen how we can use it to create passive income sources from **Youtube videos, E-books and SaaS to Courses and blogs all the way from scratch,** starting with ideation and research, creating a basic structure, generating content and taking it to marketing via email and social media.

These are tasks that would either take a large amount of your time or money and sometimes both while all you wanted to do was concentrate on growing your business, which is what you'll now be empowered to do.

Finally, ChatGPT can help you become a **superhuman freelancer**, it can cut down massively the time to do tasks such as coding, translation, ad-copy, ghostwriting and blogging.

By following the tips as well as the best practices, as Steve Jobs would say, **ChatGPT can become not just a tool, but a companion that can help you achieve financial success.**

THANK YOU!

Hi there Reader,

I want to thank you for reading this book.

I hope it was useful to you, and I wish you luck with your endeavours.

I was hoping you could do me a small favour.

If you liked the book, please consider leaving an honest review on Amazon (I read every single one).

Every review matters and your support truly means a lot.

Again, I appreciate your kind assistance.

Cheers,

Neil

P.S. Here is the link once more if you didn't grab the previously mentioned free bonus.

Included is a quick-reference description of the ChatGPT prompts from this book including access to 150+ "Act as" Prompts and another is a free copy of my "Simple Guide to Wealth"

Download it here: https://retiredecadesearly.com/bonus

AUTHORS NOTE: If you have any issues PLEASE DISABLE your browser's adblocker for this page! If that doesn't work you can email me at Neil@retiredecadesearly.com

Alternatively, scan the QR code below with your phone camera to download the bonus:

Tools I used to help write this book. (aside from ChatGPT)

JasperAI: jaspergpt.com

Printed in Great Britain
by Amazon

30077891R00066